THE OFFICIAL
ANNUAL 2020

WRITTEN BY STEVE BARTRAM
DESIGNED BY DANIEL JAMES

A Grange Publication

©2019. Published by Grange Communications Ltd., Edinburgh, under
licence from Manchester United Football Club. Printed in the EU.

Photography © MUFC.

978-1-913034-25-2

CONTENTS

WELCOME TO THE 2020 MANCHESTER UNITED ANNUAL!

As we all know, United are the biggest and greatest club in England. You might know the Reds inside out, but this is where you can learn even more.

Each of United's first team squad members is covered in detail in our profiles section – which includes plenty of little-known bits of trivia – while we also look back on the greatest moments of Marcus Rashford's sparkling Reds career so far.

You can also read all about the Manchester United Women's squad, including the new summer signings, as well as looking back on their historic first season which ended in promotion to the FA Women's Super League.

There's all of this and more besides in the 2020 Manchester United Annual. To round things off, you can test your knowledge of United past and present with some epic quizzes and teasers, before entering our competition to win a Reds shirt signed by first team squad members!

Always keep the Red flag flying high...

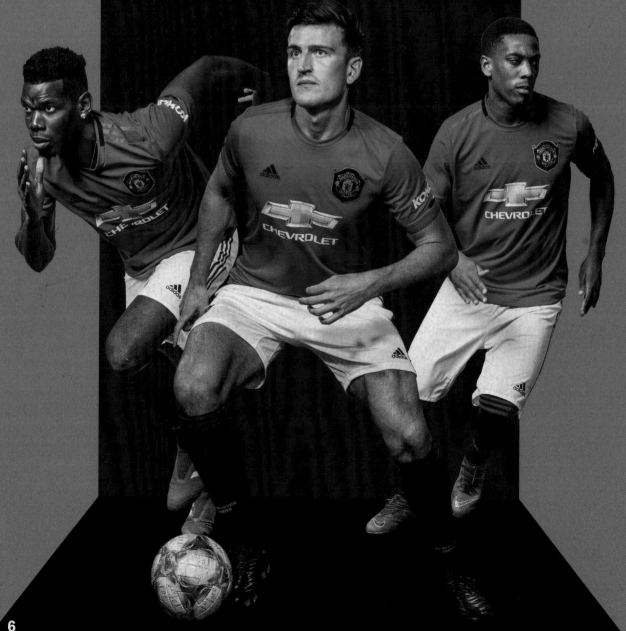

PLAYER PROFILES 2019/20

LEARN MORE ABOUT EACH MEMBER OF THE REDS' FIRST TEAM SQUAD

1: DAVID DE GEA
2: VICTOR LINDELOF
3: ERIC BAILLY
4: PHIL JONES
5: HARRY MAGUIRE
6: PAUL POGBA
8: JUAN MATA
9: ANTHONY MARTIAL
10: MARCUS RASHFORD
12: CHRIS SMALLING
13: LEE GRANT
14: JESSE LINGARD
15: ANDREAS PEREIRA
16: MARCOS ROJO
17: FRED
18: ASHLEY YOUNG
20: DIOGO DALOT
21: DANIEL JAMES
22: SERGIO ROMERO
23: LUKE SHAW
24: TIM FOSU-MENSAH
26: MASON GREENWOOD
28: ANGEL GOMES
29: AARON WAN-BISSAKA
31: NEMANJA MATIC
36: MATTEO DARMIAN
37: JAMES GARNER
38: AXEL TUANZEBE
39: SCOTT MCTOMINAY
44: TAHITH CHONG

DAVID
DE GEA

GOALKEEPER

DAVID SAYS...

"After a great save or a mistake by a defender I prefer not to shout. I am relaxed, I try to be normal after a mistake, to give confidence to them."

"To be honest, I don't think David will ever stop. He can get even better!"

EMILIO ALVAREZ, GOALKEEPING COACH

THOSE IN THE KNOW SAY...

1

 BORN: 7 NOVEMBER 1990; MADRID, SPAIN

In the space of eight seasons at Old Trafford, David has developed into one of the finest goalkeepers on the planet, with a wider repertoire of saves than any other stopper. United's four-time Player of the Year is also first choice for the Spanish national team, and his wealth of top-level experience makes him a key member of the Reds' defensive setup.

DID YOU KNOW?

David is a huge fan of heavy metal music, which he regularly tries to play in the United dressing room – often to a mixed reception from his team-mates!

ICE MAN

VICTOR
LINDELOF

DEFENDER

VICTOR SAYS...

"When people asked me what I wanted to be when I grew up, I'd immediately say, 'I want to be a footballer.' They'd say, 'Aw, that's sweet, but that's not really a job, is it?' Well, actually, it is. You just have to believe it's possible. I did."

THOSE IN THE KNOW SAY...

"Victor now understands what it takes in English football, it was similar to Vidic adapting to the English game. It's difficult and it takes time to adjust – now his class has come out."

FORMER REDS CENTRE-BACK WES BROWN

2

BORN: 17 JULY 1994; VASTERAS, SWEDEN

A ball-playing, highly intelligent central defender, Victor Lindelof arrived at United in the summer of 2017. After finding his feet throughout his first season in England, the Swedish international then set about making a name for himself in 2018/19, when he was a strong contender for the club's Player of the Season award. A class act and the coolest head around.

DID YOU KNOW?

Victor has had a huge personal announcement each year since his arrival at **Old Trafford**. He got engaged in 2017, married in 2018 and became a father in 2019. What's in store in 2020?!

ERIC
BAILLY

DEFENDER

ERIC SAYS...

"For me it wasn't difficult to adapt to life in Manchester because I had very good teammates. It's a dressing room that is like family."

"Eric is an extraordinary person and an extraordinary player. I was very lucky to manage him."

FORMER VILLARREAL MANAGER MARCELINO

THOSE IN THE KNOW SAY...

3

BORN: 12 APRIL 1994; BINGERVILLE, IVORY COAST

Though he has had his United career to date disrupted by injury, Eric Bailly has repeatedly proven himself to be an imposing presence in the heart of United's defence. The Ivory Coast international, who joined from Villarreal in the summer of 2016, is also a major figure in the United dressing room, where he is always among the banter.

DID YOU KNOW?

Even though he's a defender, Eric wears the no. 9 shirt when he plays for Ivory Coast!

ROCK SOLID

PHIL JONES

DEFENDER

PHIL SAYS...

"We've got some great footballers here. Challenging for major trophies is the vision for the players, for the staff, for the fans, everyone involved in this football club."

"Jonah thinks he's got banter but he's a good lad. He's shown that he can be a rock at the back, and he's becoming more of a leader for us now."

— JESSE LINGARD

THOSE IN THE KNOW SAY...

4 ✚ BORN: 21 FEBRUARY 1992; PRESTON, ENGLAND

One of the most experienced members of United's squad and still in his 20s, Phil Jones has won the Premier League, FA Cup and Europa League since his 2011 arrival from Blackburn Rovers. Initially deployed in a variety of roles, the England international has made his name as a brave, committed centre-back who will put his body on the line for the Reds.

DID YOU KNOW?

Phil has been a part of England's squads at the last two World Cups, plus the 2012 European Championships.

HARRY MAGUIRE

DEFENDER

HARRY SAYS...

"It's a young team and I think we've got big ambitions for the future. We've got to start winning trophies again and I'll give everything I've got for this club."

THOSE IN THE KNOW SAY...

"He's grown into someone who can lead and be a leader of men, and shown at both ends of the pitch he can be effective. He has composure and willingness on the ball as well as the ability to drive out from the defence, which I feel is as good as anyone in the game right now."

REDS LEGEND RIO FERDINAND

5

BORN: 5 MARCH 1993; SHEFFIELD, ENGLAND

As United's headline signing ahead of the 2019/20 season, Harry Maguire arrived at Old Trafford with high expectations. It took a world record fee for a defender to persuade Leicester City to part with the 26-year-old but, having evolved into one of the best centre-backs around for club and country, Harry is definitely up to the challenge of representing the Reds.

DID YOU KNOW?

Harry played for Sheffield United against the Reds in the 2010/11 FA Youth Cup final, where he came up against future team-mates Paul Pogba and Jesse Lingard.

PAUL
POGBA

MIDFIELDER

"We have to give everything for the club, for the shirt, for our team-mates and for ourselves as well because it is on us on the pitch."

"There are different types of midfielders but, in Paul's mould, there's no-one near him."

OLE GUNNAR SOLSKJAER

THOSE IN THE KNOW SAY...

6

BORN: 5 MARCH 1993; LAGNY-SUR-MARNE, FRANCE

United's World Cup-winning midfielder is one of the most gifted players in the world game. Now in his fourth season back at Old Trafford after returning to Manchester from Juventus, the Frenchman's dynamic string-pulling game is crucial to the Reds' attacking tempo. A regular source of goals and assists, Paul is a vital cog in the United wheel.

DID YOU KNOW?

In 2018/19, Pogba was the only player from outside the Premier League's top two to be named in the PFA Team of the Year.

JUAN
MATA

MIDFIELDER

JUAN SAYS...

"Juan is the ultimate professional and one of the most intelligent players I have worked with. He is a great example to our younger players in his approach. He understands what it means to be a Manchester United player."

OLE GUNNAR SOLSKJAER

THOSE IN THE KNOW SAY...

"I have been here a bit more than five years and I have realised how amazing the supporters are and especially in the tough moments. I wanted to stay, I wanted to commit to the club, to keep enjoying wearing the shirt and keep trying my best."

8

BORN: 28 APRIL 1988; BURGOS, SPAIN

The man with the most winner's medals in United's squad, Juan Mata signed a new contract in 2019 which will keep his vital experience at the club for at least another two years. A hugely popular member of the Reds' setup, Juan is universally adored and will be a key figure as United's young squad develops over the coming years.

DID YOU KNOW?

In 2017, Juan launched an initiative called Common Goal, which supports football-based charities around the world. He really is Mr Nice Guy!

ANTHONY
MARTIAL

FORWARD

"From the day I joined I have been made to feel part of the United family and I have been incredibly humbled and overwhelmed by the warmth and love of our fans, who continue to amaze me."

"I especially like Anthony. I played with him, so I know how good he is. With the right training, the right attitude and the right guidance, he's going to get even better."

EX-UNITED STRIKER
DIMITAR BERBATOV

THOSE IN THE KNOW SAY...

9

BORN: 5 DECEMBER 1995;
MASSY, FRANCE

Another exciting young forward who committed his long-term future to United in 2019, French international Anthony Martial is one of the fans' favourites at Old Trafford. His stunning range of trickery, crazily quick feet and total unpredictability mean he's capable of pulling off the most outrageous skill at any time. Opposing defenders, you have been warned!

DID YOU KNOW?

Anthony's elder brother, Johan, is also a professional footballer. Having come through the ranks at PSG, he spent time playing in France and Israel before joining Greece's Panetolikos in 2019.

15

MARCUS
RASHFORD

FORWARD

MARCUS SAYS...

"Manchester United has been everything in my life since I arrived here at the age of seven. This club has shaped me, both as a player and as a person, so it is such a privilege every time I get the opportunity to wear the shirt."

"Marcus has the mental strength and, like Wayne Rooney and Michael Owen, is mature in terms of his understanding of the game and the way he picks up concepts."

ENGLAND MANAGER GARETH SOUTHGATE

THOSE IN THE KNOW SAY...

10

BORN: 31 OCTOBER 1997; MANCHESTER, ENGLAND

Still in his early 20s, Marcus Rashford has clocked up nearly 200 appearances for United at a faster rate than almost any other player in the club's history. An increasingly influential presence in the Reds' attack, the local hero is developing into a thrilling all-round forward blessed with immense pace and power. A club icon in the making.

DID YOU KNOW?

Marcus has a huge Cane Corso dog called Saint, whose arrival in the Rashford family was marked with an Instagram post of the dog wearing a United shirt!

LEE GRANT

GOALKEEPER

LEE SAYS...

"When you come to United, you learn quickly that this is the big draw in England. Manchester United is the big club everyone wants to scalp and everyone wants to talk about. If you're on the outside, that's the club you want to pull down."

"Lee is really, really good. He's one of the guys that everybody loves, but as a goalkeeper he's really good too. It's easy for me to work with him."

GOALKEEPING COACH EMILIO ALVAREZ

THOSE IN THE KNOW SAY...

13

BORN: 27 JANUARY 1983; HEMEL HEMPSTEAD, ENGLAND

Lee Grant has performed the role of third-choice goalkeeper perfectly since his 2018 arrival from Derby County. The boyhood United fan made his debut – coincidentally against his former club – last season, and quickly showed his abilities with some fine saves. While appearances have been few and far between, Lee is a popular and key member of United's goalkeeping department.

DID YOU KNOW?

Lee is working towards a career in coaching and management, having gained a number of the relevant qualifications already.

17

JESSE LINGARD

MIDFIELDER

> "Jesse was always going to be a late developer. It was going to take him time to develop physically, but now he's a great athlete, he's quick and he can finish."
>
> PAUL SCHOLES

THOSE IN THE KNOW SAY...

JESSE SAYS...

> "I'll never take the smile off my face when I step over the line, because I know what it means to wear this shirt. I know how lucky I am to do what I do for a living, and to represent this badge, and I'm never gonna stop enjoying it for a minute."

14

BORN: 15 DECEMBER 1992; WARRINGTON, ENGLAND

Another dyed-in-the-wool Red, Jesse has been involved with United since coming to the Academy's attention at the age of seven. The tricky attacker has needed to be patient over the last two decades, but he's now a first team regular and has scored a number of key goals – including vital efforts at Wembley to help win the FA Cup, League Cup and Community Shield!

DID YOU KNOW?

Jesse's grandad, Ken, was a strongman who used to compete for Great Britain!

ANDREAS PEREIRA

MIDFIELDER

ANDREAS SAYS...

"I have spent so long in Manchester that I now regard the city and the club as my home and I'm extremely happy to continue my career here."

THOSE IN THE KNOW SAY...

"Andreas works non-stop every day in training, has a great character and knows what he has to do to continue his development here."

OLE GUNNAR SOLSKJAER

15

BORN: 1 JANUARY 1996; DUFFEL, BELGIUM

United's decision to hand Andreas a long-term contract in the summer of 2019 demonstrated the club's faith in his potential. Armed with wicked set-piece delivery and a great engine, he's a valuable weapon in the Reds' squad – as he demonstrated spectacularly in 2018/19 with his Goal of the Season winner against Southampton. Pick that one out!

DID YOU KNOW?

When Andreas made his full Brazil debut in 2018, he became the first non-Brazilian born player to represent the country in over 100 years!

MARCOS
ROJO

DEFENDER

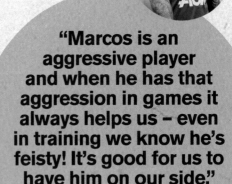

MARCOS SAYS...

"It's all about being strong mentally. I am strong mentally and I'm always going to fight hard to earn my place in the side."

"Marcos is an aggressive player and when he has that aggression in games it always helps us – even in training we know he's feisty! It's good for us to have him on our side."

JESSE LINGARD

THOSE IN THE KNOW SAY...

16

BORN: 20 MARCH 1990; LA PLATA, ARGENTINA

Serious injuries have conspired to disrupt the Argentina international's United career for the last two seasons but, whenever he's been able to feature, he has demonstrated the full-blooded defending which has made him so popular among fans. Capable of operating on either the left side or centre of defence, Marcos is a squad member guaranteed to give his all for the club.

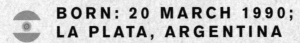

DID YOU KNOW?

Marcos is close friends with former United player Juan Sebastian Veron, who also used to be his team-mate at Estudiantes in Argentina.

FRED

MIDFIELDER

FRED SAYS...

"I'm always talking to my family back in Brazil. They're always happy and cheering me on, they're so proud of me, so proud that I've been lucky enough to play for the best club in the world."

THOSE IN THE KNOW SAY...

"He's a good player and a brilliant midfielder. Ultimately, he will do well and be very good for Manchester United. Likewise, the club will be very good for him."

BRAZIL LEGEND RIVALDO

17

BORN: 5 MARCH 1993; BELO HORIZONTE, BRAZIL

Though it took a little while for the newcomer to make regular appearances after his 2018 arrival from Shakhtar Donetsk, Fred came into his own in 2019 and showed his gritty capabilities on the biggest stages. His fine Champions League displays against PSG and Barcelona demonstrated that he can cope with any opponent, and the future looks exciting for the Brazilian midfielder.

DID YOU KNOW?

When Fred was growing up as a teenager in Brazil, United were his favourite team to control on console football games!

RED LEADER

ASHLEY YOUNG

DEFENDER

"The controller of the dressing room music, the joker of the team and probably one of the funniest guys I've ever met."

LUKE SHAW

THOSE IN THE KNOW SAY...

ASHLEY SAYS...

"You go out there as a player and you want to win, play for the badge, play for this fantastic club, which is the best club in the world. It's always about looking ahead."

18

BORN: 9 JULY, 1985; STEVENAGE, ENGLAND

The elder statesman of the United dressing room, Ashley Young has evolved with the times as a United player, developing from a versatile winger to a reliable full-back over the course of eight seasons at Old Trafford. Ashley has regularly worn the captain's armband for the Reds; a statement of his maturity and his popularity among the first team squad.

DID YOU KNOW?

Ashley likes to get a new tattoo each summer, and his 2019 close-season choice was his biggest yet: a huge effort which covered his entire back and took artists two days to create!

22

DIOGO

DALOT

DEFENDER

DIOGO SAYS...

"One day, I hope a kid comes into the changing room and says 'ok, wow, I'm playing with Diogo'. That's my goal and I think everyone's goal should be like that. You want to be a role model."

"For a young lad to come in and play like he's been here for years has been fantastic. It's great to see Diogo get up and down the pitch the way he does."

ASHLEY YOUNG

THOSE IN THE KNOW SAY...

20

BORN: 18 MARCH 1999; BRAGA, PORTUGAL

Though he had to overcome a number of injury setbacks after his arrival from Porto, Diogo Dalot had enough opportunities in 2018/19 to show that he can be a big member of United's squad over the coming years. A young, hungry defender who is versatile enough to operate further upfield, Diogo looks to have a bright future ahead of him.

DID YOU KNOW?

Diogo is very family-oriented. His mum moved over to Manchester to live with him for his first couple of years at United, while his dad flies from Porto every weekend to visit!

23

DANIEL JAMES

WINGER

"I've probably not seen anyone as quick as him in my whole career. That's a big shout, because obviously I've played with and played against some really quick players."

RYAN GIGGS

THOSE IN THE KNOW SAY...

DANIEL SAYS...

"I think every kid grows up wanting to play for Manchester United. I never thought I'd be able to play against them, never mind play for them, so it's surreal to join the club."

21 ⊕

BORN: 10 NOVEMBER 1997;
BEVERLEY, ENGLAND

As Ole Gunnar Solskjaer's first signing for United, Daniel James was bought from Swansea to bring pace and thrust to the Reds' attack. Having taken the Championship by storm in 2018/19, the Welsh international was seen as a key capture, given his ability to play on either wing or through the middle.

DID YOU KNOW?

Though he was born in England, Daniel qualified to play for Wales through his Welsh father, Kevan.

SERGIO
ROMERO

GOALKEEPER

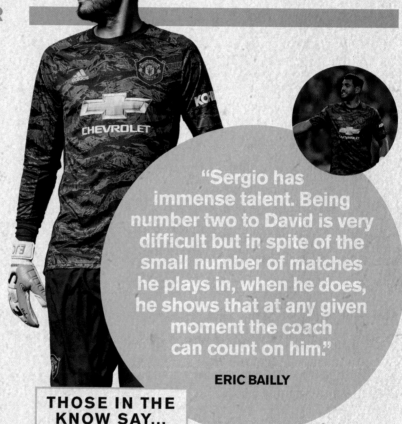

SERGIO SAYS...

"We have a great family of goalkeepers here at United, and we all make sure we put in a lot of good, hard work."

"Sergio has immense talent. Being number two to David is very difficult but in spite of the small number of matches he plays in, when he does, he shows that at any given moment the coach can count on him."

ERIC BAILLY

THOSE IN THE KNOW SAY...

22

BORN: 22 FEBRUARY 1987; BERNARDO DE IRIGOYEN, ARGENTINA

When it comes to Sergio Romero, the stats speak for themselves. No goalkeeper in United's history who has had any kind of sustained first team involvement can boast a better clean sheets ratio than the Argentinian, who has been a hugely reliable deputy to David De Gea ever since he joined United in 2015.

DID YOU KNOW?

Sergio is the youngest – and smallest – of four brothers. His tallest eldest brother, Diego, is 6'8" tall and plays professional basketball in America!

LUKE SHAW

DEFENDER

LUKE SAYS...

"This is the biggest club in the world, 100 percent. You need thick skin. You need to fight for the team, the fans, the manager and the club."

"I remember my first senior training session vividly: Luke Shaw was absolutely rapid. I couldn't get near him. He was an absolute bullet, just amazing. From that moment, I had him as a benchmark for myself, in terms of how sharp he is."

AXEL TUANZEBE

THOSE IN THE KNOW SAY...

23 ✚

**BORN: 12 JULY 1995;
KINGSTON UPON THAMES, ENGLAND**

Having had his United career cruelly disrupted by injury for years, Luke Shaw has taken huge strides towards realising his enormous potential and making the left-back spot his own. The former Southampton defender was named Sir Matt Busby Player of the Year in 2018/19, penned a new long-term deal and looks set to be a first-team fixture for years to come.

DID YOU KNOW?

Luke has regularly taken a fitness coach with him on holiday in order to stay in shape, and has also made a habit of reporting back to United for pre-season training early!

POWER HOUSE

TIMOTHY
FOSU-MENSAH

DEFENDER

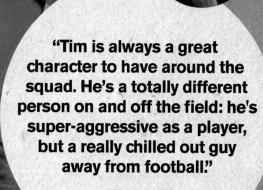

TIM SAYS...

"The Academy is strict but in a positive way for you. I think that has benefited the players. You can see it with the mentality of the players who have been through the system. It is a very good mentality to have."

"Tim is always a great character to have around the squad. He's a totally different person on and off the field: he's super-aggressive as a player, but a really chilled out guy away from football."

LUKE SHAW

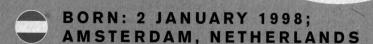

THOSE IN THE KNOW SAY...

24

BORN: 2 JANUARY 1998; AMSTERDAM, NETHERLANDS

Though he suffered knee ligament damage in the spring of 2019, Tim Fosu-Mensah has his sights set on a return to full fitness so he can resume his promising career. The young Dutch international has proven himself at Premier League level and is a versatile, energetic and sharp-witted young player who has bundles of potential.

DID YOU KNOW?

Tim was clocked as the fastest player in the Premier League during 2018/19, reaching speeds of 35.32 kilometres per hour during his loan spell at Fulham. ZOOM!

27

HOT SHOT

MASON
GREENWOOD

FORWARD

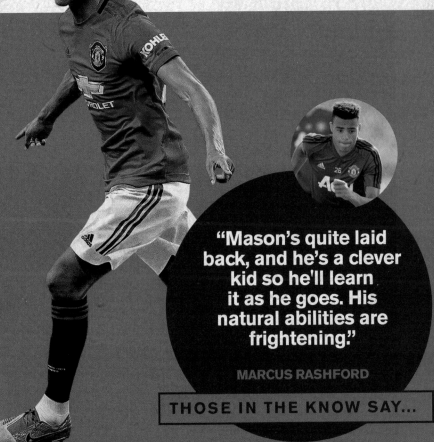

MASON SAYS...

"I just work hard on finishing after every training session. I just try and score in all the training games, so that helps me to do it in the games."

"Mason's quite laid back, and he's a clever kid so he'll learn it as he goes. His natural abilities are frightening."

MARCUS RASHFORD

THOSE IN THE KNOW SAY...

26

BORN: 1 OCTOBER 2001; BRADFORD, ENGLAND

One of the most exciting young strikers to emerge from United – and English football – in recent years, Mason Greenwood has bags and bags of potential. He's naturally two-footed, fast as lightning and deadly in front of goal. Having already been called up to the first team on several occasions before his 18th birthday, Mason might well be around the senior setup for a long time.

DID YOU KNOW?

Mason was the first player in United's history to make his debut in the knockout stages of the Champions League.

ANGEL
GOMES
MIDFIELDER

ANGEL SAYS...

"To go from being a ballboy to coming on for my debut and replacing Wayne Rooney was just amazing."

"We have some very talented young guys at the club and Angel is definitely one of them. He has great ability and a lot of potential."

JUAN MATA

THOSE IN THE KNOW SAY...

28
BORN: 31 AUGUST 2000; LONDON, ENGLAND

One of the youngest players in United's history to represent the first team. Angel is a livewire attacker who particularly excels at running with the ball, due to his speed, trickery and close control. Since making his senior debut in 2017, the Londoner has been patient in waiting for further opportunities, but his displays throughout the youth ranks and in the 2019 pre-season tour showed just how good he is.

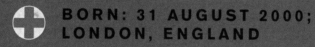

DID YOU KNOW?

Angel's godfather is none other than former United and Portugal winger Nani!

AARON
WAN-BISSAKA

DEFENDER

AARON SAYS...

"I think I will improve every step and learn different things around new team-mates. I think Man United is a big club, a big family, a big fan base, and I think they all stick together."

"I don't think I've seen anyone get the better of Aaron. You may go past him but he always manages to get a last-ditch tackle in, and you know you aren't going to win a 50-50 with him."

WILFRIED ZAHA

THOSE IN THE KNOW SAY...

29

 BORN: 26 NOVEMBER 1997; LONDON, ENGLAND

Nicknamed 'the Spider' because of his ability to use his long legs to make brilliant tackles, Aaron Wan-Bissaka is one of the most exciting young defenders to grace the Premier League in recent seasons. He topped stats charts in almost every defensive discipline in 2018/19, convincing the Reds to splash the cash for him in the summer of 2019.

DID YOU KNOW?

Aaron was a winger until the age of 19, when he was asked to play full-back in a training session at Crystal Palace. He did so well that his coaches decided he would be a defender from then on!

SERBIAN STEEL

NEMANJA

MATIC

MIDFIELDER

NEMANJA SAYS...

"I played against United many times before, so I knew it was a really big club, but when I came here I discovered exactly how big it is all over the world."

"Leadership is about getting on the field and demanding more from your team-mates and setting an example as well. Nemanja has got that in him."

UNITED LEGEND BRYAN ROBSON

THOSE IN THE KNOW SAY...

31

BORN: 1 AUGUST 1988; SABAC, SERBIA

As one of the most experienced members of the United squad, Nemanja is one of the Reds' most respected players in the dressing room. The Serbian international midfielder brings a cool, calm presence to the engine room, as well as insightful reading of the game which allows him to break up opposing attacks. He's won plenty of major trophies in the past and is hungry for more!

DID YOU KNOW?

As well as enjoying Christmas on 25 December because he lives in England, Nemanja and his family celebrate it on 7 January, as is the custom in Serbia and other Orthodox countries.

31

JAMES GARNER

MIDFIELDER

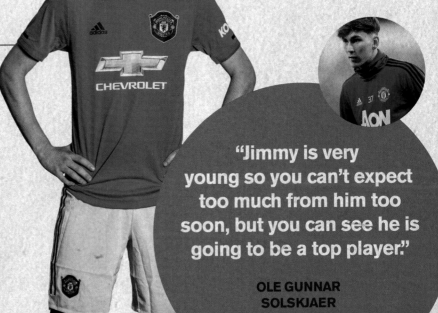

JAMES SAYS...

"The first team is what I've been working for since the Under-8s and Under-9s. You just have to keep working hard and be ready to take your chance."

"Jimmy is very young so you can't expect too much from him too soon, but you can see he is going to be a top player."

OLE GUNNAR SOLSKJAER

THOSE IN THE KNOW SAY...

37

BORN: 13 MARCH 2001; BIRKENHEAD, ENGLAND

When you're being likened to a young Michael Carrick, you're doing something right! A calm midfielder, James Garner – known as Jimmy around the club – has displayed remarkable maturity throughout his time in the Reds' youth teams. Having spent time around the first team, and scored his first senior goal during the 2019 pre-season tour, he's itching for his next step.

DID YOU KNOW?

During his rise through the United ranks, Jimmy was also captain of England's Under-17s.

AXEL
TUANZEBE
DEFENDER

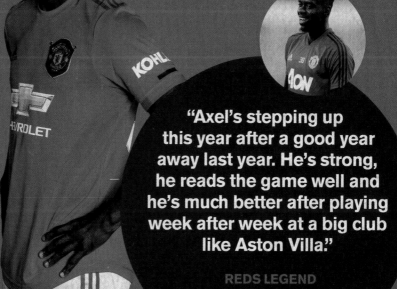

AXEL SAYS...

"I am a much better player than a year ago. I'm more mature, my decision making is better, my physicality, my ability to build myself in the game and also being a senior player."

"Axel's stepping up this year after a good year away last year. He's strong, he reads the game well and he's much better after playing week after week at a big club like Aston Villa."

REDS LEGEND WES BROWN

THOSE IN THE KNOW SAY...

38

BORN: 14 NOVEMBER 1997; BUNIA, DEMOCRATIC REPUBLIC OF THE CONGO

For Axel Tuanzebe, a sterling season's work at Aston Villa during their promotion from the Championship to the Premier League proved to be one of the best loan deals undertaken by any of the Reds' youngsters in recent years. A dominant, assured central defender who can also operate in midfield, Axel is ready and primed for a bright future at Old Trafford.

DID YOU KNOW?

Though he was born in Democratic Republic of the Congo, Axel and his family moved to Rochdale when he was a child – and he had been scouted by United's Academy by the time he was eight!

SCOTT
MCTOMINAY

MIDFIELDER

SCOTT SAYS...

"He's positive, reliable and aggressive. He's proven to his managers that he can be trusted, which is vital for any young player."

RIO FERDINAND

THOSE IN THE KNOW SAY...

"You've just got to keep working hard, coming in, doing the gym, doing the running outside, putting it in on the grass as well and going into every matchday like it's your final game for this club."

39

BORN: 8 DECEMBER 1996; LANCASTER, ENGLAND

During the course of 2018/19, Scott McTominay showed that he could cut it at the highest level, bossing the midfields of Paris St Germain and Barcelona in the Champions League. The Scotland international demonstrated his willingness to cover every blade of grass for United, while also showing his skilful passing and a useful eye for goal. A top-rated homegrown midfielder.

DID YOU KNOW?

Even though he's a first team regular, Scott had to perform an initiation song in front of his team-mates during the 2019 pre-season tour, and he absolutely smashed *Ain't No Sunshine* by Bill Withers, to a huge ovation!

TAHITH
CHONG

ATTACKER

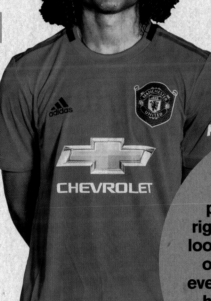

TAHITH SAYS...

"It is just brilliant to see Jesse, Marcus and Scott there in training, with the way they help me. I'm enjoying my journey and seeing what comes."

"He's just a fantastic professional. He has the right attitude to training and looks after himself really well off the pitch. On the pitch, everyone has been excited by his performances; he's an eye-catching player."

THOSE IN THE KNOW SAY...

**FIRST TEAM COACH
KIERAN MCKENNA**

44

**BORN: 4 DECEMBER 1999;
WILLEMSTAD, CURACAO**

A thrilling young talent. Tahith is tall, tricky and fearless when it comes to taking on opponents. Since his 2016 arrival at United from Feyenoord, the Dutch youth international has set about making a name for himself in the Reds' younger age groups. Having now played his way into the first team squad, the stage is set for Chong to become a regular feature.

DID YOU KNOW?

Tahith won the club's Jimmy Murphy Young Player of the Year award in 2017/18 and the Denzil Haroun Reserve Team Player of the Year award in 2018/19 – becoming the first player to win the two awards in successive seasons since Giuseppe Rossi in 2004/05 and 2005/06.

TRAINING DAYS

Whether at the Aon Training Complex or out on tour, United's players know they need to put in the hard yards on the training pitch in order to be ready to pull on the Red shirt...

HOMETOWN
GLORY

In the summer of 2019, Marcus Rashford committed his future to United with a new, long-term contract which will keep him at Old Trafford for at least the next four years. To celebrate, here are our no. 10's top 10 moments so far, as they happened...

TAKE A BOW

When Anthony Martial suffered an injury during the warm-up before United's Europa League tie against Denmark's FC Midtjylland, Marcus was given almost no time to prepare before being flung into the starting XI. He duly enjoyed a dream debut, scoring twice as United came from behind to win 5-2!

FOUR IN TWO

Three days later, Marcus was at it again. Injuries in Louis van Gaal's attack ensured that the 17-year-old had to make his Premier League debut in a huge meeting with title-chasing Arsenal. It took Rashford little more than half an hour to score another two goals, and he capped his sensational display with an assist for Ander Herrera's winner.

RECORD-BREAKER

Having established himself as a feature of the Reds' starting XI, Rashford was completely unfazed when he sampled his first Manchester derby only eight games into his senior career. As proof, it took him just 16 minutes to skip through on goal, fire home the only goal of the game and become the youngest goalscorer in the history of the fixture.

CUP WINNER

Marcus' senior career was only 18 games old when he picked up his first major honour. In a demonstration of Van Gaal's faith in the youngster, he was named in the Reds' starting lineup for the 2016 FA Cup final against Crystal Palace. After watching close pal Jesse Lingard smash in the winner, Rashford ended the season with a winner's medal!

SECOND SILVERWARE

With the 2017 League Cup final against Southampton poised at 2-2 with 13 minutes remaining, Reds boss Jose Mourinho introduced Marcus from the substitutes' bench. The speedy forward had to make a difference and duly did; playing a big role with three minutes to go as a United counter-attack ended with Zlatan Ibrahimovic heading in the winner.

5

6

STOCKHOLM GLORY

The third medal of Rashford's short career wasn't long coming. Having scored a sensational free-kick in the semi-final win over Celta Vigo, he was again named in the starting XI against Ajax in Sweden. Goals from Paul Pogba and Henrikh Mkhitaryan gave United another major European trophy, with Marcus outstanding against Dutch defender Matthijs de Ligt.

DOWNING LIVERPOOL

7

Stationed out on the left flank, Marcus terrorised Liverpool right-back Trent Alexander-Arnold all afternoon long, and his performance contained a decisive pair of goals in a key 2-1 victory. His opener – which was nominated for the 2017/18 Goal of the Season award – was unbelievable; a brilliant backheel to make space, then a thunderous finish into the far corner. Wow!

ELASTIC MAN

8

Rashford would go on to score the Reds' third goal in a thumping 4-1 win, but it was his unbelievable skill to set up Paul Pogba's opener which took the plaudits. Having superbly outfoxed Nathan Ake on the flank, Marcus left Diego Rico for dead with an elastico before crossing for the onrushing Pogba to slide home the finish. Unstoppable!

WEMBLEY WINNER

9

The sixth game of Ole Gunnar Solskjaer's interim management was a stern test, but one which the Reds passed with a huge victory, thanks to Rashford's brilliant winner. When a Spurs attack broke down, Paul Pogba's sublime through-ball sent Marcus clear, and he sent Wembley's away end wild with a measured low finish across Hugo Lloris.

HISTORY BOY

10

Never before had a team lost the first leg of a Champions League tie at home, by two clear goals, and still fought back to reach the next round. That is, until Marcus capped an unbelievable win at Paris St Germain. When the Reds were awarded an injury-time penalty, Rashford had to wait four agonising minutes before thrashing in a rocket of a spot-kick to make history.

HISTORY MAKERS

Manchester United Women were formed in 2018, with the sole aim of achieving immediate promotion to the FA Women's Super League. That mission was accomplished in style!

Manager Casey Stoney assembled a squad of, in her words: "Twenty-one strangers" but the new-look Reds instantly bonded and began notching some eye-catching wins.

United's first competitive game came against top-flight Liverpool, who were beaten by Lizzie Arnot's late winner in the FAWSL Cup, but it was the league season opener – a 12-0 win at Aston Villa – which really set the tone for the campaign ahead.

Stoney's side won eight of the first nine league games, conceding just one goal and scoring 42 times, to set a breathless pace at the head of the table. Though Durham were beaten in the League Cup, they subsequently inflicted United's first defeat of the league season in December, but that result proved a springboard as the Reds stepped their game up even further in the second half of the campaign.

113

GOALS SCORED IN
ALL COMPETITIONS

THAT'S AN AVERAGE OF
3.89 GOALS PER GAME

TOP SCORERS

TOP SCORERS

SIGSWORTH	18
GREEN	16
JAMES	17
TOONE	15
ZELEM	11

With their sights firmly set on promotion, United began the year with a 9-0 win over London Bees and never looked back. Leicester were hit for seven in February and six in March, then title rivals Tottenham were obliterated 5-1 to start a sensational run-in. The Reds went on to score five or more in each of the final five league games!

Having ultimately clinched promotion with two games to spare and won the title by nine points from Spurs, the Reds could reflect on an astonishing first season's work. "We have created not only a team but a family, and I think that shows on the pitch," said striker Jess Sigsworth, who finished the season as top scorer.

As ever, though, the celebrations quickly made way for a look ahead to the future, and United's Golden Boot winner relished the test of the top flight in 2019/20.

"We have been training to compete in the Super League and we are really looking forward to it," said Jess. "I think we have shown through our performances that we can compete. We competed and won, so we are so excited to be in that league next year."

PLAYER PROFILES 2019/20

MANCHESTER UNITED WOMEN'S SQUAD

Reds goalkeeper Siobhan 'Shiv' Chamberlain introduces each and every member of Casey Stoney's squad, shedding light on their personalities and playing abilities…

S I O B H A N
CHAMBERLAIN

G O A L K E E P E R

1

SHIV SAYS...

"I'm the most 'experienced' member of the group. Millie Turner calls me 'Mama Shiv' and everyone always asks me stuff, as if I'm Google or something. I'm always expected to know the answer to everything. If people don't know it, they say: 'Oh, Shiv will know.' Oh, and obviously I'm an excellent goalkeeper as well!"

BORN: 15 AUGUST 1983

MARTHA
HARRIS

DEFENDER

SHIV SAYS...

*"The self-nicknamed 'mini-Messi'.
Martha is a great one-v-one defender, but
she's constantly trying to score in training,
even though it's not her job. She did actually
eventually score right near the end of the season,
which resulted in one of the fans having to shave
his beard off, because he'd promised that he would
if she managed it!"*

BORN: 19 AUGUST 1994

2

LOTTA
ÖKVIST

DEFENDER

SHIV SAYS...

*"Lotta is another newcomer to the
squad who I'm really looking forward
to working with. She's quite a young
defender but she's already a Swedish youth
international, so there's no question at all
about her quality."*

3

BORN: 17 FEBRUARY 1997

AMY
TURNER

DEFENDER

SHIV SAYS...

*"A very solid, out-and-out one-
v-one defender. No-one's getting
past her. She's also my car share
buddy and she's recently got a new car,
so that's even better! She's also pleased
that we've signed another player who's
older than her, so she's no longer the
second oldest in the squad!"*

BORN: 14 JANUARY 1993

4

ABBIE
MCMANUS

DEFENDER

SHIV SAYS...

*"A new recruit. She's a born
and bred Manc, which will
help her fit in in Manchester, a
composed defender who I'm sure will
be looking forward to playing in front of
our barmy army."*

5

BORN: 14 JANUARY 1993

E L L A
TOONE

FORWARD

"Tooney absolutely loves a stepover, and if you've managed to get her to smile then you've done well. She only smiles when she's on the winning team – that's all that matters to her."

BORN: 2 SEPTEMBER 1999

7

M O L L I E
GREEN

MIDFIELDER

"Probably one of the hardest workers we've got in the squad, and she's probably the player I would say improved the most during the course of last season."

8

BORN: 4 AUGUST 1997

JESS SIGSWORTH

FORWARD

"A pure, natural goalscorer, but also another really hard worker. You always know when you're on the pitch that Jess will have your back – she's a real team player."

BORN: 13 OCTOBER 1994

9

KATIE ZELEM

MIDFIELDER

SHIV SAYS...

"The mouth of the team. If you can't see her then you can definitely hear her! She's got a great football brain as well, which gives her a really important role in the team."

10

BORN: 20 JANUARY 1996

47

LEAH GALTON

FORWARD

"In my opinion, she's the best left-winger in the country. If she can stay fit and healthy then she can go as far as she wants to. I absolutely hate facing her shots in training because they're like bullets!"

BORN: 24 MAY 1994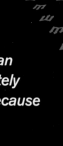

11

12

HAYLEY LADD

DEFENDER/ MIDFIELDER

"Another new member of the team but it didn't take her long to show us all how technically good she is. She reads the game so, so well. She's also our first Welsh player, so she's made a bit of history."

BORN: 6 OCTOBER 1993

EMILY
RAMSEY

GOALKEEPER

SHIV SAYS...

"I was taller than Rambo last year, but not anymore so she needs to stop growing. She's got the longest legs in the world and has massive potential as a young goalkeeper. This season will be really good experience for her."

BORN: 16 NOVEMBER 2000

13

JACKIE
GROENEN

MIDFIELDER

SHIV SAYS...

"A really exciting new signing and I'm looking forward to getting to know her more. She has excellent workrate, experience and quality. She's a World Cup finalist and a European Championship winner, so she has great pedigree."

14

BORN: 17 DECEMBER 1994

49

LAUREN
JAMES

MIDFIELDER/ FORWARD

SHIV SAYS...

"The most naturally gifted and talented player in the squad by far. She has the world at her feet if she wants it. Technically excellent, so much potential and it's so exciting to see where she can end up. She has the potential to be one of the best players in the world."

BORN: 29 SEPTEMBER 2001

16

LIZZIE
ARNOT

FORWARD

SHIV SAYS...

"Our marathon runner. She's constantly running, but when she gets on the ball she will turn opponents inside out. Left foot, right foot, doesn't matter. She's also a master baker, which not many people know!"

BORN: 1 MARCH 1996

17

KIRSTY
HANSON

FORWARD

"She likes you to think she's a quiet one but that's absolutely not the case! She's got excellent delivery of the ball. She's also just graduated from university while training full-time, which is pretty impressive."

BORN: 17 APRIL 1998

18

JANE
ROSS

FORWARD

SHIV SAYS...

"One of the quieter members of the group but the ultimate professiona She's got a lot of experience bo internationally and domestically. She'll he a lot of the younger players develop and pus on in the future

19

BORN: 18 SEPTEMBER 1989

KIRSTY
SMITH

DEFENDER

SHIV SAYS...

"Quiet, reliable and versatile. She loves to attack and will be dying to score after ending last season as the only outfield player who didn't manage to score! Sorry Kirsty!"

BORN: 6 JANUARY 1994

20

MILLIE
TURNER

DEFENDER

SHIV SAYS...

"She's a very composed defender, always full of energy. She thinks she's a magician with all her card tricks and she's definitely the joker of the group."

21

BORN: 7 JULY 1996

BENTLEY

GOALKEEPER

SHIV SAYS...

"Technically a very good goalkeeper. Fran did really well out on loan at Sheffield last year and will be looking to push on next year."

BORN: 26 JUNE 2001

22

M A R Y
EARPS

GOALKEEPER

SHIV SAYS...

"Mary's a very confiden goalkeeper who has grea ability. She will be lookin forward to returning to the FAWSL after spending last season with Wolfsburg in Germany.'

27

BORN: 7 MARCH 1993

QUIZZES & PUZZLES

IT'S TIME TO SEE HOW WELL YOU KNOW UNITED!

A

SPOT THE DIFFERENCE

Scour these two pictures and see if you can spot the six differences between them…

B

WORDSEARCH

FIND THE 10 HIDDEN REDS...

A	P	A	K	C	F	B	D	X	M
E	N	L	B	W	A	R	G	A	D
G	V	D	A	G	O	U	G	V	I
E	N	H	R	F	O	U	A	L	T
D	S	R	H	E	I	P	T	I	Q
I	A	S	L	R	A	M	A	N	S
J	A	G	E	A	C	S	M	G	P
R	S	E	M	A	J	G	H	A	B
L	I	N	D	E	L	O	F	R	F
K	G	F	U	S	K	U	B	D	E

Words go horizontally, vertically, diagonally and backwards.

DE GEA   ANDREAS   JAMES   LINGARD   RASHFORD

MAGUIRE   LINDELOF   POGBA   MATA   SHAW

NAME THE EX-RED

JOIN EACH OF THE 10 FORMER UNITED
PLAYERS TO THE FOLLOWING STATEMENTS...

1 I scored the last day winner against Tottenham which clinched the 1998/99 Premier League title.

2 I became the world's most expensive defender when I joined United in 2002.

3 I was United's first ever Uruguayan footballer.

4 I captained the Reds to three FA Cup final wins in the 1980s and 1990s.

5 I was United's emergency goalkeeper when Edwin van der Sar was injured at Spurs in 2007.

6 I signed for the Reds from Real Madrid and left for Paris St Germain.

7 I won the Ballon d'Or in 2008, becoming the fourth United player ever to win the award.

8 I was United's top scorer in 2016/17, my first – and only – full season at the club.

9 I joined the Reds from Bayern Munich in 2015 and left for Chicago Fire in 2017.

10 I became United's first ever Ecuadorian player when I signed from Wigan in 2009.

CRISTIANO RONALDO

DIEGO FORLAN

ZLATAN IBRAHIMOVIC

BASTIAN SCHWEINSTEIGER

ANGEL DI MARIA

RIO FERDINAND

BRYAN ROBSON

JOHN O'SHEA

ANDY COLE

ANTONIO VALENCIA

NAME OUR OPPONENTS

WHO DID UNITED FACE IN THE FOLLOWING MAJOR GAMES?

1. **2017 EUROPA LEAGUE FINAL**
2. **1999 FA CUP FINAL**
3. **2008 CHAMPIONS LEAGUE FINAL**
4. **1996 FA CUP FINAL**
5. **2017 LEAGUE CUP FINAL**
6. **1999 CHAMPIONS LEAGUE FINAL**
7. **2016 FA CUP FINAL**
8. **2004 FA CUP FINAL**
9. **2008 CLUB WORLD CUP FINAL**
10. **2010 LEAGUE CUP FINAL**

SPOT THE BALL

WHICH OF THESE BALLS HAS DANIEL JAMES JUST KICKED?

ANSWERS ON PAGE 61

A

B

C

D

GOAL ⊙R NO GOAL?

STUDY THESE EIGHT PICTURES OF SHOTS ON GOAL FROM 2018/19
AND SEE IF YOU CAN REMEMBER WHETHER WE SCORED OR NOT...

E

F

G

H

WHO SCORED MORE?

IT SOUNDS SIMPLE, BUT IS IT REALLY?
WHICH PLAYER SCORED MORE TIMES FOR UNITED?

 1 ROBIN VAN PERSIE **OR** JAVIER 'CHICHARITO' HERNANDEZ

 2 ANDREI KANCHELSKIS **OR** CARLOS TEVEZ

 3 ZLATAN IBRAHIMOVIC **OR** JI-SUNG PARK

 4 DAVID BECKHAM **OR** ERIC CANTONA

 5 CRISTIANO RONALDO **OR** OLE GUNNAR SOLSKJAER

 6 GEORGE BEST **OR** RYAN GIGGS

 7 NANI **OR** LOUIS SAHA

 8 DWIGHT YORKE **OR** DIMITAR BERBATOV

 9 STEVE BRUCE **OR** TEDDY SHERINGHAM

 10 PAUL SCHOLES **OR** RUUD VAN NISTELROOY

QUIZ ANSWERS

IT'S TIME TO SEE HOW WELL YOU KNOW UNITED!

SPOT THE DIFFERENCE PAGE 54

WORDSEARCH PAGE 55

A	P	A	K	C	F	B	D	X	M
E	N	L	B	W	A	R	G	A	D
G	V	D	A	G	O	U	G	V	I
E	N	H	R	F	O	U	A	L	T
D	S	R	H	E	I	P	T	I	Q
I	A	S	L	R	A	M	A	N	S
J	A	G	E	A	C	S	M	G	P
R	S	E	M	A	J	G	H	A	B
L	I	N	D	E	L	O	F	R	F
K	G	F	U	S	K	U	B	D	E

NAME THE EX-RED PAGE 56

1. ANDY COLE
2. RIO FERDINAND
3. DIEGO FORLAN
4. BRYAN ROBSON
5. JOHN O'SHEA
6. ANGEL DI MARIA
7. CRISTIANO RONALDO
8. ZLATAN IBRAHIMOVIC
9. BASTIAN SCHWEINSTEIGER
10. ANTONIO VALENCIA

NAME OUR OPPONENTS PAGE 57

1. AJAX
2. NEWCASTLE UNITED
3. CHELSEA
4. LIVERPOOL
5. SOUTHAMPTON
6. BAYERN MUNICH
7. CRYSTAL PALACE
8. MILLWALL
9. LDU QUITO
10. ASTON VILLA

WHO SCORED MORE? PAGE 59

1. CHICHARITO (59) BEATS VAN PERSIE (58)
2. KANCHELSKIS (36) BEATS TEVEZ (34)
3. IBRAHIMOVIC (29) BEATS PARK (27)
4. BECKHAM (85) BEATS CANTONA (82)
5. SOLSKJAER (126) BEATS RONALDO (118)
6. BEST (179) BEATS GIGGS (168)
7. SAHA (42) BEATS NANI (40)
8. YORKE (66) BEATS BERBATOV (56)
9. BRUCE (51) BEATS SHERINGHAM (46)
10. SCHOLES (155) BEATS VAN NISTELROOY (150)

GOAL OR NO GOAL?

PIC A: GOAL
PIC B: NO GOAL
PIC C: NO GOAL
PIC D: GOAL
PIC E: NO GOAL
PIC F: GOAL
PIC G: GOAL
PIC H: GOAL

PAGE 58

SPOT THE BALL PAGE 57

2